**Small Business**

The Pocket Guide to Strategic Planning: The 90-Day Quick Fix for the Business Owner or Manager

By Kenneth C. Bator, MBA

Table of Contents

Introduction – Page 2

I. Executive Summary – Page 9

II. The Brand of the Institution – Page 10

III. SWOT Analysis – Page 22

IV. Target Markets – Page 27

V. Goals – Page 31

VI. Budget – Page 34

VII. Marketing Mix – Page 36

VIII. Succession Planning and Training – Page 38

Appendices – Page 42

Introduction

"I'm still trying to figure out how I'm going to make payroll next month and you want me to build a strategy for the next three to five years? I'm just trying to stay alive for the next three to five weeks!"

In my years as a consultant I have heard this from more than one client. As a small business owner myself I can certainly relate. It's a catch 22: "Do I take the time to develop a strategy today or do I drive across the city to meet with that prospect one more time in the hopes I can land that business?" This is especially true when closing that sale would give your business that short-term bump in cash flow that may be sorely needed.

Strategic planning is somewhat similar to exercise in that regard. It's important but not necessarily urgent. We know we need it for our long-term health but it's very easy for a task that is clearly important and urgent, or at least perceived to be, to push our exercise or planning out of the picture. We also know, sometimes unconsciously, that our lack of exercise and planning will eventually bite us in the proverbial behind!

Managers of branches and multiple locations of larger organizations and franchises have similar concerns. While they may not have the anxiety of having to bring in enough cash flow to make payroll, as our sample statement above reflects, managers and supervisors are being asked to rise to a much higher level of expertise by their executive bosses.

No longer is it acceptable to simply be operationally efficient and run a tight ship at the local or regional office. Supervisors and managers are expected to be leaders or even mini-CEOs if you will. These new expectations often times include the following:

- Developing a specific marketing and business development plan for your local marketplace.
- Identifying and developing future leaders at the branch level.
- Cultivating relationships in the community to increase brand awareness

As a manager if the folks in the corner offices aren't holding you accountable for these responsibilities, wouldn't it be wise to stand out from the crowd and engage in these activities?

Whether you are a business owner or a manager; whether you run a retail store or a machine shop; there is too much competition in the marketplace in any industry to not create a strategy. If your organization isn't creating alignment among its brand, culture, and strategy I guarantee you have competitors that are.

The biggest hurdle is getting started and finding that time to begin building a cohesive plan. Unfortunately not every business person has the resources to attend a class on planning or to hire a facilitator to act as a guide through the process.

This Strategic Planning Guide has been designed to assist in getting over that first hurdle. First, it has been deliberately printed as a pocket guide so that you may easily carry it with you throughout your day. You may not be able to set aside a few hours in a day for planning, but you can carry this guide with you and take 15 minutes to write down an idea or two when it pops into your mind. Therefore, it is suggested that you peruse this workbook from start to finish before beginning to make any notes or fill out any sections. Doing so will make you familiar with the flow and begin to spark ideas. Then days or weeks later when a concept or strategy comes to mind you will know what section to refer to.

Second, this guide has been written in an outline format. This is in order to provide the reader/planner with a roadmap of what needs to be included in a plan and how the different items need to work together. The outline format also allows those who diligently use this guide to eventually take the notes compiled in the workbook and use it to assemble an actual written plan. As the title infers, it is expected that after carrying this pocket guide around for 90 days you will be ready to sit down and use it as a tool to write your plan.

The notes I have provided in this workbook are based upon some of the enjoyment I have had, as well as a number of the frustrations, during various strategic planning processes throughout the past two decades. Having been through strategic planning as a facilitator, as an executive, and as a member of a board of directors I have seen firsthand some of the obstacles and pitfalls that rear their ugly heads during the procedure. Most of the notes in this guide will seem like they are nothing more than common sense ... and they are. However, unfortunately what is common sense isn't always common practice.

The non-highlighted areas provide sample verbiage of how to begin writing certain sections of the plan if you choose to actually write the plan. It is expected that this verbiage will be used only as a guide and not verbatim. After all, this guide is meant to give the planner a "kick start" as well as some direction to spark ideas. It is not meant to provide paragraphs to be used verbatim. Thus, I have hopefully provided enough lines and white space to write down your own concepts and make the necessary changes to my words.

To that end, keep in mind that this workbook is *an* outline and not necessarily *the* outline. There are plenty of different formats to use to compile a sound plan. So treat this outline as such and make any necessary alterations, additions, or movements of sections to create *the* plan for your particular organization.

A "truth-in-advertising" note on the "90 Day Quick Fix" portion of our title: **there is no quick fix.** Even if you are diligent in using the guide and periodically filling out sections throughout a 90-day period to complete the workbook, at the end of those three months you need to do something with it! Nothing is more worthless than taking the time to compile a solid plan and then throwing it in a drawer or on a shelf to collect dust. Even if you feel that it's a mediocre plan – and odds are that it isn't if you truly took the time to put it together - there can still be great value in it. Many times a mediocre plan executed to perfection can be better than an outstanding plan that is executed poorly or not at all.

Some may choose to provide a pocket guide to each member of their team to use for 90 days. The team can then meet, compare notes, and use the collection of ideas to compile a plan.

Others might choose to use the guide just for themselves as leaders to compile a rough plan throughout the 90 days. They can then simply carry that guide with them to use as a reference on a periodic basis and when the focus of the business gets a little off track.

Regardless of how you choose to use the guide, remember that you need to make this plan your own in order for it to become an effective tool for you and your team. Also remember that if you discover that your organization may need more than this guide, Bator Training and Consulting, Inc. is here to help you. Simply contact us at info@btcinc.net.

Good luck and good planning!

I. Executive Summary

NOTE: The Executive Summary is usually one of the final portions of the written plan to be completed. As the name suggests, it is a synopsis of the challenges ahead for the organization and a preview of how they will be overcome. This summary is generally only two or three paragraphs in length.

_____

_____

_____

_____

_____

_____

II. The Brand of the Organization

The brand is one of the most important aspects of any organization since it encompasses every aspect of the company's being – the culture, the image, the personality, etc. Therefore, it is critical that this plan doesn't simply outline various objectives but also acts as the impetus to align the brand and culture with the strategy. It is imperative that the organization drivers are understood by management so that the brand drivers can be created in order to bridge all gaps between the foundation - such as the vision and mission - and the brand conveyors - such as the advertising, store locations and layout, and service.

Organization Drivers

The Organization Drivers – the foundation of the organization – consist of the history, mission, vision, values, and service standards. The following are the unique organization drivers of _____.

NOTE: Organization Drivers lay the foundation for the company and are the "when", "why", "where", "who", and "how" of the business.

The history is the "when" or "at what point in time" in our history we are currently. The history portion should be relatively short. At most, it is generally a timeline or paragraph on how the company was started, similar to what many organizations will place on their websites or marketing materials. This assists in developing the groundwork for the brand essence.

A brief synopsis of the organization's history is as follows:

_____

_____

_____

_____

_____

_____

_____

_____

_____

_____

_____

NOTE: It is acceptable to simply state the mission, vision, and values of the organization in the plan. However, it may make sense to write a brief one or two sentence paragraph on how these drivers were created, how they play a key role in the management decision-making process, and/or the function they play in the overall brand. This is a more critical component if the mission, vision, or values have recently been created or changed.

The mission statement:

_____

_____

_____

NOTE: The mission is the "why" we're in business. This statement should not be changed easily. The mission rarely changes unless the nature of the business is altered in a significant manner, i.e. the people the company serves has changed or the product mix is drastically different than when the business was originally built.

If your business has had some longevity, you may consider adding some verbiage to this section. A sentence or two stating how the mission lives on today from the original founders helps to tie the history to the current brand essence and culture.

The vision statement:

_____

_____

_____

NOTE: The vision is the "where" are we going. This statement is forward thinking and is short-term in nature in comparison to the mission. It is similar to a Big Hairy Audacious Goal (BHAG) and often has a three to five year life.

Some consultants argue that a vision statement is unnecessary and that the mission covers the "where" question. Even if the mission fulfills that function, the lack of a vision creates a possible lack of a culture building tool.

That tool is a rallying cry for the entire staff of the organization. Almost everyone has an innate need to be associated with a winner. Having and, more importantly, living an inspiring vision gives employees a sense of direction. It is one thing to say "We manufacture batting helmets for little leagues". However, a vision of "We will be known as the premier provider of the safest batting helmets for little leagues throughout the country" creates an entirely different mindset. If communicated properly and on a regular basis by management, a vision such as this can act as a rallying cry within the culture.

The core values of the organization:

_____

_____

_____

_____

_____

_____

NOTE: The core values listed above are the "who" we are. What do we hold dear to our core? Respect? Efficiency? Timeliness?

These core values lead to the development of the service standards – the "how" are we going to live these values.

This final piece of the brand foundation, the service standards, should be included here with a brief synopsis of how they brand the culture and service of the organization. Some organizations choose to list the service standards in this section. Others choose to refer to them in the brief synopsis and list the standards in the appendices section with a note at the end of the paragraph, such as:

(A complete list of service standards can be found in Appendix A.)

If your organization does not currently have a list of service standards they should *not* be created as an activity of a strategic planning session or as an arbitrary exercise of management. The creation of service standards should be created with all staff in order to establish support among every level of the organization. Service standards should define how a core value is displayed. For example, a value of "punctuality" might relate to a service standard of "We will return all voice mails within 24 hours".

If your institution does not have a list of service standards but plans to implement them, a brief explanation of how you plan to do so can be written here.

_____

_____

_____

_____

_____

_____

_____

_____

Brand Drivers

The service standards, along with the brand drivers, bring the foundation described above to life. The central brand drivers are the brand principle, brand personality, and the associations.

NOTE: If the brand drivers haven't already been created or defined, this represents an excellent opportunity for discussion among the leaders of the organization early in the strategic planning process. The exercise of creating these components helps not only to further define the brand but also to bring everyone to a common understanding. Even in groups where there are distinct cliques, discussion on the brand drivers generally reveals that each leader's opinion of the brand essence is very similar and sometimes even identical.

The brand principle details how the brand of the institution will be portrayed in the marketplace through various brand conveyors and reads as follows:

_____

_____

NOTE: The brand principle can be tricky for some to understand. Many times a tagline may serve as a brand principle as well. For instance, staying with our fictitious batting-helmet manufacturer example, a tagline of "For the fun of it" could also translate into marketing communications – speaking to how playing safely with this product translates into fun. A tagline like this could also be used to brand internal functions, such as having fun in the factory means adhering to safety standards.

The brand personality describes the persona of the organization as if it were an actual person. The primary traits of the institution's personality are listed below:

_____

_____

_____

_____

_____

_____

Brand associations come in two categories. First are the immediate thoughts brought to mind upon mention of the name of the company. Second are the entities that partner with the organization, or "the company you keep".

NOTE: You may choose to actually list the associations and why they are present or simply include a paragraph explaining the primary associations and how they are an important contributor to the brand.

_____

_____

_____

_____

_____

NOTE: The following are key questions that should be asked before moving on to the next section:

1. **Are the current mission and vision still valid?**

2. **Are they aligned with the institution's history?**

3. **Does the vision embrace all current realities and the intermediate future?**

4. **Do the current values and service standards still apply?**

III. SWOT Analysis

NOTE: Keep in mind that Strengths and Weaknesses are internal in nature while Opportunities and Threats refer to external forces. At least two items per section at a minimum should be listed.

NOTE: The following are some basic questions that should be asked during the SWOT analysis exercise:

1. **What is your company's unique selling proposition (USP)?**

2. **What resources does your organization have – or lack thereof?**

3. **Are competitors diminishing in your market(s)?**

4. What can potentially erode your market share?

Strengths

_____

_____

_____

_____

_____

_____

_____

_____

Weaknesses

_____
_____
_____
_____
_____
_____
_____
_____
_____
_____
_____
_____

Opportunities

Threats

_____

_____

_____

_____

_____

_____

_____

_____

_____

_____

_____

IV. Target Markets

Based upon our current target, geography, branch locations, and market opportunities the following is our market segmentation:

NOTE: This section in the outline has deliberately been left rather open and vague as target-market segmentation among institutions can vary widely based on a number of factors. Those factors include but are not necessarily limited to market size, market diversity, age of those we currently serve, number of branches, and opportunities for expansion. Simply segmenting by core and expansion markets as listed below may not be suitable for your organization. However, a core and an expansion component should be included in your segmentation process.

Core Market

_____

_____

_____

Expansion Market

NOTE: A few questions to help encourage thought and discussion when defining target markets are as follows:

1. **Which two or three characteristics create an accurate description of the entities your company currently serves?**

2. **Are there expansion opportunities present that have been identified through the SWOT exercise?**

3. **Can the organization take advantage of these opportunities without diluting the brand?**

V. Goals

NOTE: One of the primary objectives of any strategic planning session or process is to determine three to four macro goals for the organization. These "big picture" goals must be clearly aligned with the vision and other organization drivers.

Goal #1:

_____

_____

_____

Goal #2:

_____

_____

_____

Goal #3:

_____

_____

_____

Goal #4:

_____

_____

_____

NOTE: Just as the three to four macro goals must be clearly aligned with the vision and other organization drivers, the goals of the senior management team need to be clearly aligned with these "big picture" goals. Likewise the goals of middle management need to be spawn from the goals of senior management and so on throughout the other levels of the organization. This process of alignment, what I call "org-chart goal setting", begins to create accountability among all staff and begins enhancing the culture to initiate the execution of the plan.

Depending upon the time allotted and the size of the senior management team, the goals for each department executive can be created during a strategic planning session. It can also be done immediately following the strategic planning session as a mentoring exercise among the owner or manager and the leaders of each functional area. Regardless, the senior management team goals/departmental objectives should be listed in this section of the strategic plan along with a narrative on how the goal setting process will be executed throughout every level of the institution.

One particularly effective way to illustrate the alignment between the macro goals and the departmental goals is to list the senior management objectives under the each corresponding organizational goal.

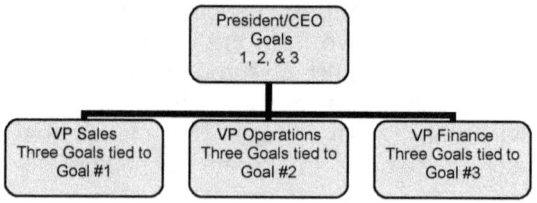

VI. Budget

NOTE: It would be useful to have a draft of a workable budget for the upcoming year, or at least a finalized budget for the current year, to use as a guide during the strategic planning session. After the discussion on goals, a dialogue on the budget can produce a dose of reality as to what is truly achievable. It can also create a positive energy of how resources can be allocated in order to take advantage of opportunities in the market place.

The annual budget should be included in this section in the final version of the strategic plan along with key assumptions. It is acceptable to include the full budget in an appendix if necessary and simply discuss essential components of the budget as well as how resources will be allocated in order to achieve the goals

Creating a budget can be a challenging endeavor for some. This is especially true for those busy business owners with companies not quite large enough to hire a CFO or accounting manager. That is probably the case with only 80% or more of small businesses. However, many bookkeeping software packages, such as QuickBooks, contain budget and cash flow functions that will help. While there is space for some budget notes below, many times it is easier to include the budget in an appendix.

_____

_____

_____

_____

_____

_____

_____

_____

_____

VII. Marketing Mix

NOTE: This is the section to include the actual marketing plan. Some companies choose to list the marketing plan as an appendix. Philosophically, not including the marketing mix in the heart the strategic plan erroneously labels this function as one that is less critical than others. More important, since the achievement of some or all of the goals listed above will hinge on the successful execution of the marketing plan it is essential to include these marketing initiatives in the body of this document.

The marketing plan should be created after the strategic planning session, or after the organizational goals have been set, by the marketing team and then included in the final strategic planning document. Much like the goals, it is critical that the marketing plan is completely aligned with the organization and brand drivers discussed above

Most small business owners and branch managers will not have a marketing team, or even one marketing professional, to assist in compiling this section. Regardless, this is a key section to complete. At a minimum, the basic marketing and business development activities that will be undertaken throughout the year should be listed. Including a narrative on how all of these marketing tactics will be executed in a unifying fashion to achieve the goals would also be wise.

_____

_____

_____

_____

_____

_____

_____

_____

_____

VIII. Succession Planning and Training

NOTE: This section is not always included in the final strategic planning document. However, succession planning and training are important components to the future viability of the organization. Plus, the achievement of the macro goals listed above may require the execution of specific initiatives from this area.

The following is one format to use to define the succession plan for each key position:

Position _____

Possible Successors:

    1) _____

    2) _____

    3) _____

Skills that each potential successor possesses that are required to fulfill the responsibilities of the position above:

1) _____

_____

2) _____

_____

3) _____

_____

Additional training and development necessary, including estimated date of completion, in order to prepare each successor for the position above:

1) _____

   _____

2) _____

   _____

3) _____

   _____

For obvious reasons, it may be wise to exclude this section from the plan for copies given to staff and possibly some management positions.

Some organizations choose to list specific areas of training that are planned for the coming year for staff, specific departments, and management teams. Similar to the marketing plan, the leader of HR may want to create and include a detailed plan for training and development. This would be particularly important if training is discussed in the goals and/or values section

As eluded to earlier, for those business owners that serve as the head of human resources – as well as the CEO, CFO, COO, CMO, CIO, and any other C-executive you would like to mention – you may want to just list some basic items here. For instance, an owner of a car repair shop may list how the junior mechanic will be trained on rebuilding a transmission before the end of the year or how his son will be groomed to take over the business in three years.

Similarly, branch managers may discuss how certain employees will be cross trained at their location. Specific needs such as a new part-time cashier can also be listed here.

APPENDICES SECTION

NOTE: Appendices can include, but aren't necessarily limited to, service standards – as mentioned earlier and listed below, regional data, market information, product mix, marketing and event calendars, and any other supporting documentation. Usually information that provides credence to a section of the plan but will take up several pages of space is best to place in an appendix.

APPENDIX A – Service Standards

APPENDIX B – Regional Marketing Data

APPENDIX C – Event Calendars

APPENDIX D - _____

ABOUT THE AUTHOR

Kenneth C. Bator, President of BTC Small Business, has over two decades of experience in helping organizations make money, save money, and just plain surviving. Over his career as a management and marketing expert he has served as an executive of three different financial institutions throughout the country and has assisted several small to medium-sized businesses to reach new levels of effectiveness.

As an independent consultant, Ken Bator has facilitated several training and strategic planning sessions for many organizations since 2001. Bator has earned a BS in Finance and an MBA in Entrepreneurship from DePaul University as well as a Certificate in Integrated Marketing from the University of Chicago. His articles have appeared in many trade publications including The Credit Union Journal and ABA Bank Marketing.

Learn more about BTC Small Business at www.btcinc.net, a subsidiary of

BATOR TRAINING & CONSULTING

www.ingramcontent.com/pod-product-compliance
Lightning Source LLC
Chambersburg PA
CBHW072301170526
45158CB00003BA/1146